VERSES OF A JAMAICAN FARM BOY

Donald E. King

"All rights reserved. Copyright © 2019 by Donald E. King. No part of this publication may be reproduced or transmitted in any form or by any means, without permission in from the author."

ISBN 978-0-578-49698-0 (softbound)

Copy Editor: Lisa King
Design: Lisa King

THE AUTHOR

Donald King was born in Jamaica in 1937. He grew up on a farm in St. Andrews Parish with two brothers, Hermon and Bentley and a sister Barbara.

While there he came to be a talented track athlete and competitive sprinter. His mother Iris King became the Mayor of Kingston, and a steadfast humanitarian in both Jamaica and New York where she eventually relocated. Donald has also lived in Britain and New York; he now resides in Summerville, South Carolina.

He has been married twice and has six beloved children.

Donald has been writing short stories and poetry for most of his life. Although his eye site has been reduced to shadows, he continues to write.

This is his first published book.

This Book is Dedicated
to My Brother and
Friend Hermon King.

Firebird

CONTENTS

Introduction to the Author	3
Dedication	5
A Painter I Would Be	11
Imagine Machine	13
Tomorrow, They Die	15
The Cane Cutters Woman	17
Father	20
Running	22
Her Umbrella	24
Island Home	26
I May Never Know	28
Brothers Three	30
Eyes of A Vagabond	32
An Old Man's Daydream	33
She Was A Painter	35
Where the Albatross Flies	37

Scarface And Me	40
The Angel	42
Farm Boys	45
Nubian Diana	47
A Face at The Window	49
The Air Is Free	50
Coming To South Carolina	52
Heart to Heart	54
For Iris	57
A Brave Heart	58
Woman for Thee I Sing	60
The Boy That Went Away	61
Beyond My Mind	64
Outlaw Comanche Woman	66
Mother	68
The Journey Begins	70
Sister Selene	72
Firebird	74

Lady of The Night	75
Lament	77
If Only You Had Not Sailed	79
Color Her Blue	80
The Battle We Must Win	82
I Wonder	84
On A Park Bench	86
Earth Mother	87
Your Soul Is A Hero	88
Tender Moments	89
Annie Mac	91
Wondering Star	93
The Angel of Death Watches Over Me	95
Running with Race	97
Come Home	99
Sacred Love	101
From the Shadows	103
Mind and Soul	104

The Seed	106
A Candle Burns Low	108
Angela King	110
As I Live and Die	111
Never Again	112
The Blues	115
Dream Angel	116
The Journey Begins	118
Hot Tears Are Mine	120
I Will Sleep No More	122
Africa	124
Citation Page	127

A PAINTER I WOULD BE

So many beautiful things in this world,
Such loveliness and perfection.
So many sights and sensations,
Like starry nights
And true love
That will never die.

I wish my words
Were the brush
Of a great artist.
I would mix and stroke
Brilliant paintings across your mind.
Splash the colors of my love
Alive in the magic land
Of my imagination.
A universe of canvases
To delight your senses.

As long as my heart beats,

I give you my gifts.
And every breath you take
Will be immortalized
Upon my canvas.

IMAGINE MACHINE

Love evermore,
A dream of fools and saints.
Love, the imagine machine
The Marco Polo of the heart's universe.

When it is betrayed,
Pain, another traveler
Becomes embedded in its tender flesh.
Then tears come to soften the blow.
Tears never a more faithful servant,
Sweet water to bathe the heart
To sow the seeds of spring.

When pain dies, as it must,
A butterfly will emerge.
Does the soul of pain weep?
Or does it sift through the ashes
Looking for charred memories of a dying love?
Like a thing with a dead child

Called Devotion.

She realized, at last,
We are only slaves of time,
And time has no love, no mercy,
And no reason.

TOMORROW, THEY DIE

Drums vibrate,
Ten thousand heartbeats
Of living sound
Fill the African night.
Warriors rise, fall
And swirl like a bonfire.
Feet pound the earth
In the dance of death,
For the holy juice
Has vanished fear.

Within darkened huts,
Mothers pray for strength,
Send words from their hearts
With lips to the sky,
And chant the ancient lament.
"Dance my son, my child,
Tomorrow hot blood
Will flow cold."

"Through the ages,
We walked among the fallen.
When the killings were done
Held pierced flesh to our bosoms.
Cried for our daughter's duty
To raise more sons,
And take our place
At the graveside."

THE CANE CUTTER'S WOMAN

In the heart of the mangrove swamp,
Flies breed in dead things.
Bubbles ooze from fetid soft and slimy mud,
Air is rank with rotten sweetness and salt.
God's sun burns the night and turns it into a
        sparkling day.

A pot boils bush tea.
A man rises, stiff and sore,
His pallet is thin and lumpy, smelling of stale
        sweat and unwashed sex.
Last night's rum furring tongue and mouth, head
        throbbing a painful beat.
He covers his nakedness with patched clothing.
In a pool of stagnant water behind the hut,
He relieves himself as fiddler crabs scurry away.
Cornmeal porridge, a chunk of bread and
        breakfast is done.

His woman puts more bread, some salted fish, a
    half ripe mango in his pouch.
Lunch is served.
No words are spoken.
Words are useless as yesterdays discarded banana
    skins.
A brutalized love sleeps uneasily between them.
A touch, a rueful smile and he is gone into the
    sweltering morning,
A Machete strapped to his back.

She looks at her reflection in a clear pool,
Lusterless eyes stare back.
She rubs dry skin,
Pokes at a drooping breast,
Feels a rounded belly.

Tears rush to her eyes,
She remembers her dead children.
Falls to her knees and wails,
Begs God again for mercy.

The one in heaven is silent.
The one gone to cut cane
Is relentless.

FATHER

My father was strong,
Stronger than any man,
And big.
He filled the earth
With dignity.
His touch,
Power in sensitivity.
A symphony of solitude
In his eyes,
Shone the secrets of forgiveness.
The wine we drank was sweet,
The vineyards were rich.
Yesterday,
When he was here
In the aroma
He left behind,
In the shadow of his smile.
I remember
The abundance

He so freely gave,
And asked
No man for naught.

RUNNING

I am running,
something hungry howls
At my back.
I am desperate, angry,
The thing has no reason,
Is deaf, blind and ravenously hungry.

I am running,
The thing ate my youth,
And is now gnawing away
As a dog with a bone
At the rest of my life.

It is a sirens song
Burrowing into my flesh,
It laughs at my hearts futile fighting.
I am an addict to
The sound of death.
I put the remnants

Of my hopes and dreams
In a sack on my back,
And run as a stag
Before the hounds.

Then I saw you running,
I heard the screams
Inside your head, see panic
Shining in your eyes.
Come, take my hand,
Together we may find
Shelter and grow strong.
I'm weary of endless flight,
Let us turnabout,
And tilt at the monster
With the lances of our salvaged dreams.

HER UMBRELLA

I remember, I remember,
The day I knew
My love had found another.
A leopard became my mind,
A prowling silent shadow.
Rumbling in his throat,
Unsheathing his claws.
He became the king of my soul.
For years he hid behind
My curtain of fear and pain.

On a rainy day in May,
I stood watching the gutter,
Staring at the city's grime
Running down hungry drains.
Gentle fingers brushed my arm,
"You're getting wet," she said,
"Would you like to share my umbrella?"
Something flowed from her eyes and smile.

Her touch,
Cool water to a desert traveler
Thirsting on burning sands.
The leopard knew his time had come,
He curled up upon himself
And was gone.

We became eagles she and I,
Soaring between earth and sky.
And felt the wonder
Of being close forever.
I still dream of the night
We danced naked under the stars,
Calypso music washed over us.
We worshiped a pagan god.
She wore a hibiscus in her hair,
Sea winds blew the secrets
Of wild blossoms on her skin.

ISLAND HOME

Oh, misty seas of life,
Where is my island home?
Where do I lay my head to rest
On this fair and tranquil shore?

Are the forests tall and cool?
Are the rivers sparkling and clear?
Will the valleys and glades comfort my soul?
Will the fields be as shimmering gold?

Is there contentment in the sunlight?
Is there happiness in the air?
Joy on the wings of the wind?
Love in the fibers of my heart?

And in the morning will I behold the Most High
In the majesty of my towering mountains?
In the song and beauty of birds and rose?
Will I be given the humility to praise Him?

For in the vastness of my universe
I've met the faces of despair,
Of desolation, fear, and loneliness.
But, never the face of God.

Oh! Misty seas of life.
You are a demanding mistress
Whom I will desire to see no more
When I go home.

I MAY NEVER KNOW

My mind's aglow,
Aromatic with memories
Of past encounters.
My body's a stranger,
Engulfed by sensations
Of hope and desire.

I gaze longingly
At the portal
Of your soul.
Remote, yet sweet
With the aroma
Of your touch.
And I smile
At wonderful eyes.

I am terrified
To reach out
Lest you frown,

And wrinkle the brow
I long to kiss.
Worse, far worse,
Lest you laugh,
And deeply wound,
The tender shoots
Of budding love.

BROTHERS THREE

When we were young before responsibility called
    our names,
We ran wild and free, we were a team,
Hermon, Bentley, and me.

Though in later years we were sometimes oceans
    apart,
Our bond remained a living thing.
We respected all men and bent our knee to none.
After marriages came and went,
We turned our faces to the setting sun.

Bentley broke our hearts
When his valiant heart failed him.
We gave his ashes to the sea
As befits a true Mariner.
A passing ship tooted a farewell message to him.
There will come a time when we will be together
    again,

In a land of pure sunlight.
A place where yesterdays and tomorrows are not
>	even a whisper on the eternal wind.
And where the rage in our fighting hearts will be
>	extinguished at last.
We will roam this land, young and free once
>	more.
Still within our bond of the finest gold.

Brothers three,
Into eternity
Hermon, Bentley, and me

EYES OF A VAGABOND

He is a stranger who walked the streets on wobbly
        legs and broken shoes;
And he looked at me through eyes of blue and
        gray, with flecks of gold.

He held out a shaking hand,
With cracked nails that demanded the contents of
        my purse, and my conscience.
And when I did cross his palm with coins,
He went to the tavern door.

With wobbly legs and broken shoes, he looked
        back at me;
Through eyes of blue and gray, with flecks of gold.
And in them,
I could see,
Remnants of his pride adrift in an ocean of regret.

AN OLD MAN'S DAYDREAM

The mantle of old age
Wrapped around fading eyes,
Watched meadow grass and wind
Dance their turbulent dance,
Fresh, powerful, forever young.

I felt ugly,
As ugly as muddy water
Befouling life's clear stream.
Gone are the days
When I was a swallow,
With summer breezes
Warm on my face.
With youthful love songs in my mouth.
Hot blood in my veins,
The world was mine.
My wild and carefree days
Won no prizes,
But, I gave freely of my heart

And cared for my fellows,
I take pride in that now.

I hope someone will be there
To hold my hand,
And share what's left of my love
When I am dying.

SHE WAS A PAINTER

She did not lie,
She did love me, in her way.
I was a dreamer, she an artist
With a need to paint, with her velvet brush so
      fine.
Putting the colors of Autumn rampant into my
      body.
When she was done,
She stayed awhile
To admire her creation.
Then her need arose to find another canvas
And she simply went away.

My soul became a field
After the locusts have gone,
Numbed by the devastation.
My heart came crashing down
Like a tree in a forest fire.

Consumed by a searing pain only a forsaken lover can feel.

WHERE THE ALBATROSS FLIES

Looking through the eyes of youth, the road of life
       was a fabulous thing.
It stretched beyond my imagination,
It promised me beautiful dreams.
I would be an albatross flying high in the heavens.
I could not wait to sample life's treasures,
But dark shadows emerged.

When I first sampled the joys of womanhood,
I held in my arms,
A creature of soft, beautiful wonder.
She easily betrayed the sweet magic I felt.

When she spoke of love, the truth hid its face in
       shame.
A sweet honied mouth held a forked tongue.
I met many like her along my path,
Amidst the lies, cheating, and betrayals
I too lost my way.

Then, there were times when I flew like the
    albatross again.

Coming upon an oasis
On life's rough and rocky road,
I met a woman there
Whose inner beauty taught me the meaning of
    true love.
There is a line in a famous poem that I hold
    passionately inside my soul,
"Write me as one who loves his fellow men."
    (*Hunt, 186-*)
Through all the anger and violence in my
    unbridled life,
I have always reached into my heart.
When time had cooled my passion,
I sent a little love to those who reviled me.
For the goddess, I truly worship demands this.

Men call her many things,

For me, she is the embodiment of everything that
> is love,

For she is the Queen of Heaven.

And I have never broken faith with her.

The light at the end of the road beckons to me
> now,

When it finally reaches out and embraces me,

I will go with my head held high.

SCARFACE AND ME

I just laid to rest the last of my kin,
The worthless scrub lands we tried to farm, broke my heart and took their lives.
I am now taking the trail to where old men and horses go to die.
Scarface will know the place to lay us down.

I remember the wild years of riding a stagecoach shotgun,
Blazing trails on the Pony Express.
I remember the bodies lying on the ground after an Indian raid.
Many men and women, even young tender ones were laid to rest.
Countless mounds of dirt mark their trail as they wended their way towards the western sun.
I helped hunt outlaws,
I killed men only in a fair fight,

I lived a hard life upon a hard and unforgiving
> land.

Scarface has laid down now, for this is where our
> trail ends.
I knew he was dying;
I held his head in my arms and stroked his face.
"I wonder my old friend," I asked him,
"Will they sing for folks like you and me who
> blazed the trail for those to come?"

THE ANGEL

Sleep vanished from my mind,
When the sound of slobbering and wailing cut
　　　through my dreams
Like a sharp knife.

I opened my eyes,
An angel stood there shining like a star,
It burned my senses to look upon her.
To describe her beauty went beyond the
　　　boundaries of my tongue.

At her feet, a man knelt,
His hand covering his face,
He was sobbing like a child,
At times, a loud cry burst from his lips.

"I have come to warn you." a voice in my head
　　　said,

"You are trespassing beyond the sphere of your
 conscience,
Beware you do not venture too far.
Look upon the man at my feet,
When the Creator's light was shone upon him
He became as you see him now."

"Who can give him peace?" I asked.
The magnificent light filling my world spoke
 again,
"You can" came the reply.
"He can make your harvest bountiful if you would
 only listen."
The angel spread her wings and disappeared.

"What can I do to ease your pain?" I asked the
 weeping man,
"The pain I feel is a rapturous joy filling my heart
 to bursting," he said.
"For I have received the light."

"If you do not cleanse your mind, we will both
> perish,
For I am your soul and your conscience."
Then he too vanished.

FARM BOYS

We, the farm boys of yesteryear grew up tough,
Our friends had mostly empty bellies and dirty
       clothes.
And girls whose morals I suppose,
Lay at feet that wore no shoes.

We never flinched from curled lips
And open sneers.
We fought in the streets
For those outnumbered by the privileged classes,
Who, from their lofty heights bore down on us.
We fought for what we believed was right,
We fought because we were imbued with the
       blood of a mother who was one in a
       million.
Wherever she laid her resplendent love down
Among the poor and disenfranchised,
Her name still lives on.

We were taught never to flinch or quail,
And so, through the years we have marked her trail.
We took blows that put us down, my brothers and I,
But, got back on our feet and remained resolute.
Yesterday's memories will forever remain remarkable
Because of the things we stood for.
I hope the green rolling hills that are tomorrow's dream,
Await us when we travel on.

NUBIAN DIANA

The maid could run,
Oh, how she ran
From love.
Swift as a swallow,
Mountain water never ran so sweet.

She laughed as she ran,
Silken, pussy willow laughter,
Reaching the moon
And touching the clouds,
Filling the night with music
Like a firefly swarm.

As hunters loosed their bolts
She caught them with enchanted hands,
Pulled some from her body
Laughing at the blood,
And dancing on the dark wounds.

She wrapped that body
Around their frustration,
Filling them with wonder.
All that was left in their hearts,
Was an empty room of broken promises.

A FACE IN THE WINDOW

Within the gray stones
Of depression,
A rune spirit,
Shuffles in dank darkness.
Seeking a portal.
Unseen bars
Stronger than fear,
Impervious to hope,
Guard the keep.
He climbs stairs without end.
Relentless despair,
A crushing demon
Astride his back.

THE AIR IS FREE

Like fine sweet rain,
The musk of promised love
Evermore filled the chambers
Of her heart.

Then the stiletto of betrayal
Bit deep into the very core of her,
Far into the silent stillness
Within the halls of her soul.
There, tender clouds wept
In the dark night,
Through countless phases
Of the moon.
Yet still, she remained unclean.

In time, she extracted the blade,
And ugly scars closed the wounds.
Breathing in all her courage,
She turned her face

To the stars,
And exhaled sweet pain
As a child from her womb.

COMING TO SOUTH CAROLINA

As a stranger, I came,
To a rich land.
Flowers so lovely,
Rivers so gentle,
Cool forests, bountiful sea.

But the song of the south
Is a wary lady,
Part Valkyrie, part magnolia
She holds in her hands
Echoes of happiness and pain.

I asked to dance
To the music of her
Spiritual kingdom.
Perfect eyes smiled,
"If you are true, be welcome."
With the hypnotic mystery
Of an opening rose,

She comes to me now,
One sweet sensation at a time.

HEART TO HEART

The look in your eyes
Said so many things,
Perhaps you want more
Than I have to give.

If it is my body on your mind
It is yours,
I've given it before.
Don't be surprised,
It is not as fragile as it seems,
But is my gift to you
If that is what you want.
The only key you'll need,
Is under the mat
Outside my front door.

If it is the key to my heart you seek,
That will not be so easy to find.
A stranger came into my life,

From behind the curtain of my dreams.
Came as warm against my skin
As sunlight in the morning.
He was an endless sea,
Waves of him sweetly
Lapping the shores of my heart.
My love just melted
Right into his beautiful music.
He had nothing but pity
For my foolish heart.
And it came back
Battered and bruised.

I am afraid of eyes like yours.
In dark places
The flowers are dying my dear.
The hummingbirds have fled,
The geese gather by the pond.
Autumn's colors that were
A most brilliant quilt a moment ago,
Are turning brown on the cooling earth.

But how he had dazzled me,
In the spring of my youth.
A rose at first blush he was,
Tender and lush as new grass
After the rains.

Here in my winter room,
His memory is the embers on a fire
That once warmed my heart.
Just as you want to now,
In the springtime of your youth.
Like when I first kissed his mouth.

FOR IRIS

'Twas only a dream ago,
Her God and pilot
Called her home.
But the purity of her love
Ever constant and true,
And the glorious light; her star of morning left
      behind,
Will always be with us.

Oh, to see our golden girl
In her wings and shining robes.
A lustrous jewel at perfect peace,
In the embrace
Of her beloved Savior.

We miss her terribly,
But never mourn.
We hold her memory in our hearts,
For she is truly happy now.

A BRAVEHEART

I remember the velvet night
We danced to the music of a country band.
Your eyes sparkled like diamonds,
Pearls glowed at your throat,
And that flaming red dress you wore blazed in the
        ballroom light.
You were a sight to behold,
Truly magnificent,
But you were so frail.

The horseman called Death rode his pale steed
        hard through that tender body;
Before he took your life.
Tonight, was your way of spitting in the hungry
        eyes
Of the relentless death rider.

I was so proud to be your partner
Out there on the dance floor.

Then he won my darling.
That vile and damned creature came one dark
        day,
And stole you away.
My life became an empty place,
When the only true light it had ever known
Was extinguished from my world.

Your memory is a melody
Playing on sweetly in my heart.
And as long as I shall live
It will never, ever stop.

WOMAN FOR THEE I SING

Sing praise to the God who created thee "woman".
He anointed thee with sacred oils,
Making thine eyes depthless with wondrous
        promises;
Thy mouth, sweet instrument men dream will
        sing unspoken,
Eternal love songs into their thirsty blood.
Breasts that glow in the darkest night.
Inner fires calling the chosen.
Hold me close for I am the key;
Thine heart, mysterious as the universe,
An altar, pagan and holy.
Keeper of secret desires.
A divine river traveled to thy beloved, precious
        oasis;
A golden veil called El Dorado.

THE BOY THAT WENT AWAY

As a young man,
I went away to breathe
The air of distant lands.
The moon spoke
To my mind and heart,
Put the taste of wanderlust in my mouth.
Made me see foxfires
Dancing like sirens
On the horizon.
I wanted to fly as seagulls fly
And kiss the open water
Dark and deep.
Sleep in the arms of mountains
Tall like craggy fingers,
Pointing at the stars.
The call was irresistible
And so, I traveled.
There is a wonderful
Everlasting silence in my head,

But I still hear
The voice of the earth,
Strong and noble
Touched with a mother's love,
And the song of the sea
Sweet as a woman is sweet,
Deep in my heart.
I never tried to turn and take
The path home.
There were times,
When the longing
For familiar places
Encircled me like a hungry serpent,
And my step faltered.
But a rainbow
Rose with the dawn,
Whispering my name.
And if I could fulfill my dreams,
I would die
With the sun
On my face,

With the wind
At my back,
And the soul of the sea,
Wrapped around my body
For a burial shroud.

BEYOND MY MIND

To the people of this world like me,
Only aware of total darkness
Few cry useless tears.

Behind the lids of eyes,
To some, there is an endless beauty,
In the forever night.
There is an eternal canvas,
On which to paint the masterpieces
Locked away in their minds.
Every sunrise and sunset,
Are delightful to behold.
It is a joy to compete
With the wonders of nature.

Sometimes we can paint
Our own universe,
And sit among the stars and blazing comets.
Then with the power of our imagination,

Hold the earth in our arms,
And fill it with the compassion
It so sorely needs.

OUTLAW COMANCHE WOMAN

We have traveled many miles, my wild cowboy,
They call you outlaw,
You never told me why.

We have left my tribal land and the people of my
 blood.
My love for you is as strong as yonder mountains
And burns like a fire within me.
We have come through wind and rain hiding by
 day and traveled by night,
For your Comanche woman knows the darkness
 well.

We are always just ahead of your posse men,
Traveling south to the river you said you would
 make us free.
Now we're overlooking your Rio Grande
Shining like a silver snake in the morning sun,
But your posse men are upon us.

Their eyes are filled with hatred and their guns
    are angry.
I can go no further; I must tarry here.
The child we made together cannot wait to leave
    my body and I grow weary.
My trail ends now.
I must do what Comanche women have always
    done when the tribe is threatened,
I will hold them here until you cross your
    freedom river.

So, ride beloved of my soul,
Do ride hard, and do not look back.
We shall meet again where buffalo roam once
    more
On the lush prairie fields of the Great Spirit
In his perfect sky.

MOTHER

A Queen she was to those who knew her heart,
A clipper ship sailing the oceans of our lives.
To those who called her name, she unfurled her sails,
Giving of all her love and substance.
There was a time when the need for her was so great,
That she held the City of Kingston in her ever-loving arms,
And did what the Creator asked of her,
From a well that never ran dry.
We, who have always drunk from her cup of compassion, understanding, and self-pride,
Beseeched of Gabriel, Master of the divine trumpet
To fill the skies with his wonderful music of welcome.

So, the heavenly host may know, Iris Winifred
        King has come among them.
Blow it long and sweet for her Master Gabriel,
We implore this thing of thee,
Blow it long and sweet for her.

THE JOURNEY BEGINS

And Mary said to her son,
"Your hour has come,
I told you it would.
Go forth and bring divine rain
to a world dying of thirst.
Ugly are the minds of men;
The forests of the world
Are but a thicket
Compared to the evil
Lurking within them.
It is the path you must travel
If you wish to save their souls.
They'll see your miraculous deeds
And hear the wondrous words
Of love, forgiveness, and mercy
In the message you bring,
From a father beyond the stars.
As a woman,
I have known glory.

As a vessel,

I was made exalted.

As a mother,

I'm filled with rapturous pain.

Hold me in your arms once more

Before you go,

My son, my son,

My beautiful son."

SISTER SELENE

A ghostly curtain
Across the windows of my existence
Flows tranquil, in its given place.
A chilled face,
At perfect peace
Smiles gently.
Into nothingness, she glides,
Graceful in eternal sleep.

To touch her eyes,
To kiss her pale cheeks,
To let my tears moisten
Her barren smoothness.

Look upon this goddess,
Reflecting the glory of Apollo,
Whose heart lays beating
On the altar of her captivity.
His glow of love

Warms her.
She smiles compellingly,
Sweetly savaging the hearts of men.

If only her departed soul had stayed
And given her a taste
Of laughter and happiness,
And the wonder of love.

To the adventurous,
She is bewitchingly impossible.
To the lost,
A beguiling comfort.
To the lovers,
A challenge to ecstasy.

She floats serenely
Men call her the moon.

FIREBIRD

I remember you so well my little firebird,
I admired you in my youth.
You strutted and ruffled your feathers
And shone in splendor,
A living torch dancing around our berry bush.
It was as if death could not touch you.
I arm myself now,
With your celebration of life.
It is a shield for my heart and mind
Against the reaper of souls.
In the final battle,
I will weaken and give ground,
But, as long as I can wield the sword of life,
I will battle the agents of death
with my memory of you.

LADY OF THE NIGHT

She reached out breathing estrus,
Knowing her pray.
My mating instinct burst into flame,
Caution and decency
Blew away with the night wind.
She had a greasy face, knowing eyes and a fixed
    smile,
Under a predatory brow.

I didn't care.
We locked in electric passion,
A raptor ascending
A mouse.
Blood as white-water rushing.
The sex of her,
A pagan altar
Drinking the seeds of life.
I rose, a dazed thing, with blank eyes and dry
    mouth,

Elated yet ashamed
Amid drained daring, and empty pockets.
Her eyes shun,
A wet tongue darted,
She smiled
A little victory in her unending quest.

She melted back into the shadows as a spider would,
A mighty instrument of deliverance and commerce,
Primed, ready and waiting.
For a while, the earth was rich,
The grass as sweet and soft as eiderdown.

LAMENT

A gentle firestorm from her
warmed up my heart.
My desire was fueled to madness
In her tender arms.
We made wild and wonderful love,
I drank deeply of her angel sweetness.

Then along came a Mockingbird,
With dazzling eyes and astonishing plumage.
Kisses honey sweet,
She sucked all reason from my brain,
She tore at my soul
With songs of savage beauty.
And I lost my way.

My angel opened her wings,
And I fell to the earth.
Cries of regret
Died on a winter wind.

The wound would not be salved.

I stood on the river's edge,
Watching her fly away.
My eyes ran with bitter tears
Every time she lifted her golden wings.

IF ONLY YOU HAD NOT SAILED

Oh Columbus, Columbus,
If you had only
Stayed your ships.
So much blood
Red, pregnant, and rich,
upon the African Veldt
Did run in the wake
Of your caravel.
So many voices
Forever silenced,
By the wind in your sails.
Tears of innocence
Died at sea and in foreign lands.
And unkind hands crushed to dust,
The bewildered hearts
Of tender souls.
Oh Columbus, Columbus,
If you had only
Stayed your ships.

COLOR HER BLUE

Her lover fell into
The abyss of another
Woman's arms
And is forever lost.

You can see
Pain locked in sadness
Behind her eyes.
She cries for his tender touch
To soothe her aching wound.

Weep for her
All you jilted lovers
With tears left unshed.
Weep for the blue lady,
For no one should be so alone.

If the moon could cry
Its tears would fall beside

The tender tombstone
Of a love that died.

She is a song
With a tortured heart,
An angel with a broken wing.

THE BATTLE WE MUST WIN

Listen well my comrades,
The enemy is a vandal of the soul,
He's diseased, unguarded hearts' for Millenia.
In nations large and small
His blows broke our hearts,
And tore our flesh.

The final conflict has come.
He stands across the field
Brought to bay our courage.
He still sneers, but I smell his fear
Like a fine wine.
It's been a long time coming.

"General Martin Luther,
General Martin Luther.
What is it, captain?
There is a man,
Riding a painted horse

With a magnificent war bonnet upon his head.
His people, he says, cry vengeance."
"Send him to the fore captain,
Send him to the fore,
He'll be our standard bearer
For valiant is his heart,
True courage his shield".

"Come, my rainbow warriors
There is no turning back,
Unleash your love, your valor,
Your compassion.
Drive them into the beast
Again, and again.
Though your arms ache,
And your lungs burst,
Show no quarter.
Let no man, woman,
Or a child of you waiver,
Nor any sect, color or creed".

I WONDER

He walked the fields,
His blood runs bittersweet.
Anticipation and apprehension fill his blood.
Meanwhile, hawks circle lazily overhead.
The aroma of wildflowers fills the gentle wind.
Tomorrow when the sun rises,
She will come to him
And pour the wonder of her body all over his life
    once more.

Their time together will be short, here in their
    cabin love nest.
He who has promised to love and cherish her
    waits in another world.
She comes with the morning
And the beauty of her fills his heart to bursting.
They fill the hours with lovemaking,
Sweeter than the spoken word is their hunger for
    each other.

He wishes this world would never end.
They whisper love everlasting, and they cling to
      each other in the wonderful aftermath.

At sunset, he is alone again,
His soul walks in a rain cloud
Wet cold and so alone.
His mind reaches into his memory of the power of
      their lovemaking,
He wonders with a heavy heart,
Does she make his body burn
With the same passion, she puts in his
When they make love?

ON A PARK BENCH

She sat alone.
Wisps of gray hair
Bobbing in the breeze.
Vacant rheumy eyes,
Wounded by hope
Accused the world.
A tiny bird, melodic,
Startlingly alive
Fluttered by.
Thin lips smiled,
Perhaps a fleeting memory,
Awoke and slept again.
Then she rose
And walked away.
Tall and erect,
Proud and defiant,
Twilight was falling softly
All around.

EARTH MOTHER

Beyond, way beyond the stars,
Where yesterday goes home and tomorrows
      embryo grows
Sweet on the vine.
In the gardens of God,
In the eternal fires of heaven's forge,
She was conceived.
The strongest iron cast,
A golden heart to rule the stardust in her soul.

I saw her in my mother's eyes,
Proud and strong.
Feared sword aloft,
And compassion her companion.

When hell on earth opens its gate,
She girds her loins,
Flies into battle unflinching,
For she is woman.

YOUR SOUL IS A HERO

When you love is lost in the dark veil of betrayal,
And your strength is but a feather in the wind;
The wells behind your eyes have run dry,
In the center of your soul is a hero called courage.

Release the guardian out of the dismal darkness.
A messenger will come;
A virgin unfurling sweet dreams to soothe your
      aching heart.
Tender tendrils will grow once more within your
      garden walls.

TENDER MOMENTS

She looked at the playground
Eyes wide in wonder,
The world awaited the sound
Of her first footsteps alone.
With a brave smile at me,
An adjustment of her bag,
She walked into the sea of faces
And didn't look back.

I watched her bobbing curls
Slender neck and shoulders,
And wondered why God gave girls
Into the hearts of fathers.

She joined a long line
And walked into the assembly hall,
I left her alone for the first time
In the company of strangers.
All day I wondered,

What if she cried and cried?
What if, what if? I pondered.
But I have come to understand
Little girls are braver than their fathers.

ANNIE MAC

We did not see
Our guiding star,
Slipping beyond the Horizon.
She fell in blessed silence,
Drifted away
In soft splendor
Like a leaf in
An autumn wind.
Even though we knew
Her passing would
Enrich the heavens.
Our grief knew no boundaries,
For she left behind
A legacy of such beauty
The like of which
may never come our way again.
She was our beacon home
When we strayed
In the darkest night.

She was our champion
Giving endless strength.
You could see the love in her eyes,
Feel the compassion
That came from her soul,
And her smile reached across
A crowded room
And touched only you.
Around the campfires
Of our memories,
We will always hold dear
The essence of her spirit.
And remember our devoted friend,
Our gentle warrior,
Our Annie.

WANDERING STAR

On the eve of All Souls Day,
When wild geese flew across the moon;
Something pulsed in my blood,
Touching my soul with St Elmo's Fire.
I knew until the day I shall fall
And become dust,
Soiling the soles of men's shoes
I must follow the wild one.

I was alone in your world,
Full of frightening promises with expectant faces,
And where the truth yet remained a virgin.
My spirit longed to be free,
Beyond the horizon was a diamond mine waiting
      to be discovered,
Stars had hearts beating liquid fire.

Now sometimes when laying on my back, among
      fields of ripening corn,

I write love letters to you across the golden
        softness of a full moon.

Even in the sweeping majesty of the high sierras,
I have held you close.
Making love on the banks of deep, dark canyons
Beside white water running rampant.
My foolish heart longs for the nearness of you,
Whenever I stumbled, exhausted and lost, your
        spirit lifted me.

Please understand beloved husband,
The call of the wild one was irresistible to me.

THE ANGEL OF DEATH WATCHES OVER ME

The storms of life
laid waste a hopeful heart.
Stars fled my eyes,
Years stole my youth
With not so gentle fingers.
Joy withered,
Promises became dry rivers.

I prayed,
But the rains did not come.
Vultures looked down,
Circling always circling,
Patient as death.

In my middle years,
I wandered in hell.
Then I came upon a like spirit,
And our souls touched.
The estuaries behind our eyes,

And in our hearts
Overflowed.
Oh, how we dreamed of a new Eden.

Then, silent as an owl's shadow
Gliding over a moonlit meadow,
Death took her away from me.
I sought and begged for God's mercy
to ease this nameless pain
but could not find it.

RUNNING WITH RACE

She is always there,
Amid the tumbling music.
Inside the promised lands
Of my heart and loins;
When I look at her,
Inhale her scent,
I am immortal.

The taboo of race blows cold between us,
It laughs at our romance.
"I may be ugly," it said,
"But I too hunger for love.
I am like a woman longing to give birth,
Except I am unclean".

"Come dance with me in the dark,
And find my icy beauty,
As many have in my shadowy places,

Dance with me,
Or be damned forever
In the eyes of my disciples."

COME HOME

You were the noble wolf
Of my wilderness.
When you went away,
Love in all its eloquence
Traveled with you.

I sit by the campfire
Of your memory now.
And remember the wild stallions
That raced across the meadows
Of my heart and soul
As you held me close.
Now at night,
The wind whispers your name
In the willows outside my window,
I yearn for you.
Come home my darling,
And I'll be the dream
Before you wake in the morning,

The cloud upon which you sleep.
When you reach for me
I'll be a velvet glove
Stroking your desire.

SACRED LOVE

Deep Scars
On the fabric of her heart
Lay sleeping
In bittersweet memory.
Like tears shed without meaning,
The essence of her being,
Strength and compassion
Looked at the world
With defiance and love.

My mother,
Stands astride my yesterdays.
A gentle giant,
A timeless molder of my clay.
She hid her pain
Behind her eyes,
While she nurtured the bruises
Of youthful folly.
And in the maze of life,

She ofttimes
Carried me in the arms
Of remembered lessons.
No one knew
The shadows of her soul,
Only the bonds of love
She spun from within hidden places,
That coiled around our hearts
And endured.

FROM THE SHADOWS

In his youth, he fought to the rhythm of a lustful
    heart,
For glory in the back seat of his father's car.
Soon after he bathed in the sparkling dew of the
    grass;
He remembered how he disguised his eyes,
And his lies breathed fearless insincerity.
He pretended his life away.
Refusing to surrender his armor lest he perish.

He remembered fuel injected women of distant
    nights,
That consecrated his demons in the heart of
    battle.
He wondered how much of his memory was like
    clotted blood,
Bloated remnants of life running no more.

MIND AND SOUL

There have been times in the past,
When the reservoir of rejected thoughts
High in the mountains of my mind,
Threatened to burst and cascade maliciously and
        with barbarous intent.
To ambush and overpower my reason,
To disrupt the sanity of my thinking.

The thought of having to seek deliverance
And salvation from myself,
If I allow this stagnant pool
To bathe my conscious mind.

Of discovering that my pious and virtuous
        conscience,
Finds it incredibly sweet
To have intimately encroached,
With the forbidden, loathsome morass
Tormenting my hunger for the truth.

A tempting serpent to my doubt,
And a majestic sorrow for my depression.

THE SEED

Tears like hot butter
Ran down her cheeks
And she trembled
With rage and shame.
She raised her eyes to heaven
And cried her desolation,

A voice came from somewhere,
Anywhere, everywhere.
"If you look past your pain,
You will find a seed
That is my love.
Nurture it with care and tend it,
With time it will grow
Abundant with fruit.

Put the seeds of the fruit in your mouth,
And in your eyes and ears.
Sprinkle them among

The highways and byways
Of your life.
Give them to strangers,
To friends and enemies alike.
And soon your world,
Will know the meaning
Of true love".

A CANDLE BURNS LOW

Sometimes she walks out into the desert
When the night time surrounds her world,
And replays in her mind,
The dream that she had of him.
The moon that once glowed and filled their tender
        moments,
Now shines cold on her.
At times coyotes sing their lonesome song,
It rises to the sky
And when it comes back to earth,
It wraps itself around her body.

A distant train cleaves the night,
Wailing, wailing, wailing,
Rushing headlong through the darkness.
Once the morning sun begins to rise and paint the
        sky,
The bird's song drifts across the sand.

She leaves the place that has become her kindred
> spirit
And heads for their once happy home.

Despair is not just a word,
It is a thing with no heart or pity,
Riding her soul night and day.
It encircles their bed like a serpent.

"Come home my darling, come home to me.
Come home before this creature devours my will
> to live."

ANGELA KING

Something divine came to earth,
Soft and as sweet as moonlight.
Covering her eyes with dreams,
And her heart with wishes.
Took its breath of gold
And painted her soul with gentleness.

We look skyward now,
Past starry nights sublime,
Into the corridors of eternity.
Her star of grace is there,
Floating in serene beauty,
Along the boulevards of heaven.

AS I LIVE AND DIE

Dewdrops are liquid butterflies,
Seeds of purity,
Strewn in fragile beauty upon the morning of my
      life.
Phantom trains wailed the sweet pain of the blues
      into my soul.

When I became a man,
Wishes and promises of my former life
Now lay under tender gravestones;
They died in the heart of this dreamer.
Tears of regret lie cold and bitter on my hollow
      cheeks;
For lost loves and departed years.

NEVER AGAIN

I had been out with friends and we had been
>   drinking.
My angry woman plunged a hot naked barb into
>   my foolish heart.
I lashed out in a moment of alcohol-infused
>   madness.
In dumb disbelief I watched the women I had
>   loved nearly all my life,
Walk out the front door.

In the morning, the cold hands of reality entered
>   my fogged mine.
I tried to tell myself she would be home soon
And be my sweet love of the past forty years,
All over again.

But unbearable days past.
Family and friends could not find her,
The police, the hospitals could not help.

For weeks, the wind blew cold in my soul,
I could not remember the last time I ate or slept.
I thought I would go insane.

One dark February morning as I was watching the
        falling snow,
I faintly heard the door open and close behind
        me.
Two wonderful arms enfolded my body and a
        voice I would die for said
"I cannot live without you,
Could we start again my darling"?
The sound of her voice
And the touch of her hands,
Were the most pleasing moments that happened
        to me.

I swore at that moment
To the universe and beyond,
This woman,
This body of my body,

This heart of my heart,
Would never want for love again.

THE BLUES

The blues is your heart and soul deeply wounded.
The pressure of the melancholy,
The hopelessness, the dull unending pain,
And malady.
An unbearable burden,
Pressing down on your spirit.

For the lucky and the strong,
The winds of spring will blow again
And roses will bloom once more.

For the unlucky and weak,
The cold arms of winter
Will carry their spirits
Into the valley of despair.
That rages on for all eternity.

DREAM ANGEL

The green leaves of summer swayed, fluttered and
      danced.
The breeze was filled with rose and jasmine.
He did not see her coming until she was in front
      of him.
Her beautiful face smiled hello
And he knew in a second that she was the dream
      angel,
That had turned his nights into magic for so
      many, many years.

He turned and followed her,
Watching her walk was unreal.
Like seeing a swan glide
All effortless, grace in motion.
His heart became a bass drum
An alto saxophone played on his skin,
Guitars strung sweetly somewhere in his blood.

He caught up with her,
And told her, never before had his world been so beautiful.
"I've loved you in my dreams.
My prayers have been answered. I have found you at last."

Her smile was gentle,
His dream angel raised her left hand to his face
And he saw a band of gold.
"I am so sorry," she gently whispered and walked away.
He let his tears flow free and watched,
As his dream angel disappeared from his eyes.
An angel with a broken wing.

THE JOURNEY BEGINS

And Mary said to her son,
"Your hour has come,
I told you it would.
Go forth and bring divine rain
to a world dying of thirst.
Ugly is the mind of man,
the forests of the world
Are but a thicket
Compared to the evil
Lurking within.
It is the path you must travel
If you wish to save their souls,
They'll see your miraculous deeds,
hear the wondrous words of love,
Forgiveness and mercy,
In the message you bring
From a father beyond the stars.

As a woman,

I have known glory.
As a vessel,
I was made exalted.
As a mother,
I'm filled with rapturous pain.
Hold me in your arms once more
before you go,
my son, my son,
my beautiful son."

HOT TEARS ARE MINE

The stars fell upon us,
They fueled our fire as we danced
Weightless and free upon the mountain tops of
       the moon,
And dove with reckless abandon into whatever
       sensation called our names.
We revisited and investigated until total
       exhaustion
Wrapped us in the sweetest of blankets.
And when duty to husband and family called her,
Our parting was lingering and delicious.
The sun would rise and set only a few days before
       our loving would explode again.
And how we would delight in each other once
       more.

As she made her way home,
They put a knife into my lady
Her money ran away with her blood.

She took the temperature of the pavement
Into herself.
Sightless eyes stared into the farthest dark.
The wind moaned,
And the trees swayed,
And I realized desire
With a broken heart.

I WILL SLEEP NO MORE

Oh! Fly, fly away death,
I need more time,
I have found a reason to live.

For many long years,
I sat like a stone in a brook,
Watching insects breed.
I slept in the arms of content,
And woke up amid the pages of a great writer.
Something tender and beautiful began to make
      love to me;
She is my pen.

How wonderful it is to find such joy,
I must become worthy of her.
She warms my heart as the river never did.
She makes me feel like my dreams can walk the
      earth.
That I may look up one day,

And see diamonds
Falling from the sky.
Then I said to her
"I'm at peace."

AFRICA

My grandmother once told me, there were ancient gods living in the wind blowing the length and breadth of Africa. Men call them Mariah and Sirocco, and many other names, but their real names are known to only a few. They blew across the veldt, on the rain forests, up and down mountains like Kilimanjaro, from timeless Egypt to the mighty Horn. And if I went and called to them with a pure heart, they would come to me. They would fill my senses with their aura and teach me dances as old as time. Tell me of golden kings who once ruled vast kingdoms. Touch me with a magic that would allow me to walk among lions and fly with the flamingos.

She said they would recognize the lineage of blood coursing through my veins and could trace it back to ancestors who lived even before the ice age.

Instead of filling me with awe, pride and longing, the story terrified me. I felt there was not a worthy bone in my body to undertake such an awesome pilgrimage.

Now fifty years later, I am contemplating a trip to the mother country, whose scattered children have felt the yoke of every evil. When I walk upon the land of my fathers, I will go into the bush and pretend it is her bosom, prostrate myself and kiss her tear-soaked earth. "Mother", I will say, "know that this foolish, prodigal heart has always loved you".

CITATION

Hunt, L. (186-). Abou Ben Adhem. https://www.poetryfoundation.org/poems/44433/abou-ben-adhem

www.ingramcontent.com/pod-product-compliance
Lightning Source LLC
Chambersburg PA
CBHW020301010526
44108CB00037B/464